Experience the Power of a Poem! ™

Cock-A-Doodle-Doo

100 Morning Haiku

Brian J. Mueller

DIGITAL ALPHABET BOOKS

Cock-A-Doodle-Doo

100 Morning Haiku

*Your patient endurance
will win you your lives.*

Luke 21:19

Table of Contents

Dedication.. vii

Haiku (俳句) ix

Introduction xi

100 Morning Haiku xiii

Bonus Haiku 103

Acknowledgements................................ 127

About 128

Also by Brian 129

Notes.. 130

Dedication

To those who awaken in the middle of the night
and find comfort at the dawn.

Haiku (俳句)

Haiku is a type of short form poetry from Japan. Traditional Japanese haiku consist of three phrases that contain a 5 / 7 / 5 pattern of phonetic sounds similar to syllables. Haiku was given its name by the Japanese writer Masaoka Shiki at the end of the Nineteenth Century.

Haiku today are written worldwide. The haiku in English typically employ different styles and traditions while still incorporating aspects of the original haiku form. In Japanese, haiku are printed as a single line, while haiku in English often appear as three lines. Haiku are conventionally about nature. There are several other forms of Japanese poetry related to haiku, such as the tanka.

*Adapted from the Wikipedia entry for *Haiku*.

Introduction

I once coveted opportunities to speak. I'd be glad to chat with one person, or better yet address a crowd. I had a lot to say and believed that others needed to hear me.

Something has since changed inside of me. My eagerness to speak and be heard is much diminished. I often feel as though I've been pounded by the ocean surf for years and simply need some time to catch my breath. At other times, I prefer to listen because my story, or that same old tale I've been telling all these years, is no longer interesting. Maybe I've finally realized that people who look like me have done all the talking for far too long.

Despite my personal evolution, I do have a few things to say and share with others. My now considerable life experience has given me a bit of potent wisdom. Yet I still fear saying too much. Then I stumbled upon a book of haiku, collected from another poet's regular online postings. These tiny poems intrigued me and gave me the idea to write some of my own haiku. Writing in this short form of poetry opened the possibility for me to share thoughts and feelings without getting lost in words and unnecessary detail. Haiku allows a poet to rely on the reader's imagination to bring the words more fully to life.

The haiku in this collection were written during the early days and weeks of the Covid-19 Pandemic. It was a time of uncertainty and fear. It was also a brief period when so many of our assumptions about life, including how it should look and what we accepted as true were laid bare. Everything about my own life was suddenly open to questioning. And though many of the haiku in this collection come from a place of uncertainty, they also point the way to new possibilities.

In the stillness of many early mornings, I noticed my soul just sitting there patiently waiting for me to become silent before sharing these short poems...

Blessings,

Brian

- June 1, 2022

100

Morning Haiku

1.

Good morning to you,
intrepid wanderers all.
Let's go chase the sun!

2.

Every breath you take
is a greeting at the door
of Rumi's guest house.

3.

Allow mystery
by letting go of your plans
one day at a time.

4.

The stars in your eyes
confirm the fire in your soul.
Set the sky aflame.

5.

A good God is one.
A loving God becomes two.
A shared God is three.

6.

Stiffness in my neck,
a rumbling in my stomach,
dawn comes too early.

7.

I hear a small voice
asking me countless questions.
I have no answers.

8.

Come community.
Teach me the power of more.
Awaken my heart.

9.

We are all artists
gifted in some divine way
with a unique love.

10.

You seriously
need to look in the mirror
and have a good laugh.

11.

One of those mornings
when I wake and think fondly
of my comfy bed.

12.

When too serious,
just remind me I too am
a troublemaker.

13.

Don't start at the end.
The beginning is better.
Your soul holds the seed.

14.

Look at that building.
Even it slowly crumbles.
All will dissipate.

15.

The long dark shadow
where you've been hiding your gifts,
cast by the divine.

16.

There's much more to you
than the bones stacked together
in a human frame.

17.

Neither here nor there
We are led by the unseen
to where we belong.

18.

A knock at the door.
Well hello, it's the virus!
I expected you.

19.

I think everyone
has at some point in their life
asked aloud, "Why me?"

20.

Let's be subversive.
Pretend what you know is wrong.
Has anything changed?

21.

Let's talk about God.
Better yet, we can listen
as God speaks to us.

22.

There are survivors
who show us the way forward
no matter the odds.

23.

Self-sufficiency
is almost without meaning
when two are present.

24.

I hold ideas
at odds with one another
in liminal space.

25.

Data is one thing,
bad judgement a second,
the absurd a third.

26.

Maybe we are light
cast into the universe
by a dying star.

27.

If you hold your breath
you won't be able to speak
when God comes calling.

28.

Don't ever give up
your fierce struggle to let go.
Boom it will happen!

29.

Pause for a moment.
You have all you can handle.
That's more than enough.

30.

Look in the mirror
until you see what God sees
peering back at you.

31.

I would say anger
fuels the fire burning in me,
but love keeps me warm.

32.

I carry the tears
of fathers and grandfathers
who came before me.

33.

A routine ain't bad
if it includes a few friends
and something to drink.

34.

Give me a moment.
I find myself on both sides
of this argument.

35.

Play the lottery.
Or do what the wealthy do
and own all the banks.

36.

Alone in a room
and there is only one door
- so many choices.

37.

It's so frustrating
not knowing what I don't know,
aware of something.

38.

Releasing the past
is the only way forward
in an unjust world.

39.

Standing on that ledge,
a diploma won't help you
decide what to do.

40.

What you see and hear
is only the beginning
of the true story.

41.

Here's the difference
between a man and a boy:
time, surrender, love.

42.

It's probably true,
most of us love the people
much more than the church.

43.

If you go outside
everything gets much better,
even your writing.

44.

Whatever came next
was always waiting for you,
though you were clueless.

45.

I took off my watch.
It was not telling me much
but the time of day.

46.

When you do nothing,
you begin to recognize
little must be done.

47.

Shoot the arrow high.
It will still return to Earth,
like your precious life.

48.

Who provides the fire?
The light and heat are needed
for our conversion.

49.

Where's the talking stick?
There's something I want to say
when the time is right.

50.

What's in that backpack?
It looks extremely heavy.
Why not take it off?

51.

I open my heart
and slowly begin to see
I am not alone.

52.

It's not who you know,
rather making space within
for whomever comes.

53.

What are you thinking?
This, that, and the other thing.
Why is it you ask?

54.

A cracked shirt button
isn't worth the time to fix.
Trust me, I've tried twice.

55.

I wear them so well
I'm afraid to take 'em off:
anger, resentment.

56.

Nothing seems to be
what it first appears to be,
not even our life.

57.

What if everything
you knew to be absolute
blew away one night?

58.

Don't try to fool me.
The way you say I love you
is pure poetry.

59.

There is no other.
A day will surely come when
you awaken whole.

60.

Begin to gather
yourself in meaningful ways,
at this time and place.

61.

I'm not in the mood.
My patience is exhausted.
Let the fire burn out.

62.

The big lie today:
outright individualism.
Wake up and come home.

63.

My eyes drift westward.
The dusk awakens my fears.
Come the reckoning!

64.

There is no person
considered on all accounts,
not needing some work.

65.

No one ever knows
the power of a secret
until it is told.

66.

Who are you kidding?
Going back will not save us.
Nor will more effort.

67.

Too many big words
obscure the real meaning.
The heart speaks simply.

68.

Don't forget your lines.
You've been rehearsing for years.
The audience waits.

69.

Fear sits near my core.
Right beside it sits my love.
Neither wants to budge.

70.

Always consider
forgiving yourself before
accusing others.

71.

Fall and keep falling.
There's always further to fall
in your quest for ground.

72.

Whatever you burn
with the fire inside your heart,
stays burnt forever.

73.

It's gonna be fine
if you'll just admit defeat
and try something new.

74.

We witness in awe
Earth's magnificent beauty
and become human.

75.

The circuit goes pop!
We wonder what just happened
in total darkness.

76.

I have less to say
the greater I understand
my desire to speak.

77.

I haven't come here
because I have the answers.
Rather I need help.

78.

Let's take a day off.
Must we do something right now?
Let's see what happens.

79.

Pull that tiny thread
and watch this world unravel,
you along with it.

.

80.

It takes away breath,
then takes away lasting fear
as it frees your soul.

81.

Go to the water.
But don't settle for a drink.
You must get all wet.

82.

Something different
would be for me to seek help,
and to accept it.

83.

When life is too much,
resist the urge to escape.
There's nowhere to hide.

84.

I want nothing more
than to connect with the source
of eternal love.

85.

We can all get lost,
blown off course into darkness
by life's swirling winds.

86.

What is mine to do?
I deserve my attention.
Self-love opens me.

87.

It's always something.
To which I nod and reply,
"Always something else."

88.

Look a bit closer.
What is it you are seeing?
Do you need more time?

89.

First open your heart.
Next start exhaling slowly.
Here comes the release.

90.

It is easier
to think of lines in four beats
than five-seven-five.

91.

My humility,
imperfect though it may be,
sets my spirit free.

92.

First it's, God help them!
Then it's, Oh God you devil!
Last it's, God help me!

93.

Life is effortless
when all effort is shifted
toward loving life.

94.

I can see you there
but I am afraid to move.
Won't you come to me?

95.

Tell me what you know
or what you think you now know.
Tell me anything.

96.

I'm glad you know it.
Many others know it too.
But it won't save you.

97.

You think left to right.
But those who hold the power
think top to bottom.

98.

Why did you come here?
Oh, that's an easy answer:
to write and provoke.

99.

I remember you.
What have you returned to say?
I can hear you now.

100.

Go beyond anger.
I'm sure you'll find a sadness
you hid years ago.

Bonus Haiku

101.

Cock-a-doodle-doo!
The dawning age calls to you.
Cock-a-doodle-doo!

102.

Grief is a lemon
too sour to eat all alone.
Love is the sugar.

103.

Bird of fine feathers,
aware of his true beauty,
with soul full of pride.

104.

Suffering exists.
Your suffering is real.
Home is where to heal.

105.

"I saw that rock move."
"Impossible," you reply.
"I saw it," I say.

106.

Human reasoning
can one day make a forest,
and burn it the next.

107.

Temptation is great
to avoid pain at all costs.
What a waste of time.

108.

Get out, get out now!
The fire is out of control.
Can't you feel the heat?

109.

Is it November?
Or is it still October?
Don't ask the weather.

110.

Why do you refuse
to open your eyes and see,
bearing fierce witness?

111.

Resist the grindstone.
It sharpens your base instincts,
then unleashes them.

112.

Endless days and nights
ruin your imagination,
and incite world wars.

113.

Go ahead and laugh
- louder, until your sides hurt
- with sincerity.

114.

Take psychology.
Also take theology
and philosophy.

115.

You had the whole truth
by the tender age of ten,
nothing left to learn.

116.

The last to exit
as a body is dying,
the immortal soul.

117.

Chugga-chugga-chug.
The train rolls along the tracks.
Chugga-chugga-chug.

118.

Before lecturing,
me or anybody else,
discern your reasons.

119.

Here at middle age,
something inside cracks open.
Out pours poetry.

120.

Hooli-Booli-Ba!
Why must all make sense to you?
Or even to me?

121.

Everything, it seems,
is brittle at the edges.
Can the center hold?

Acknowledgements

Creativity is never a solitary endeavor. Even though I wrote these words, laid out the book and designed the cover, it would not have been possible without the tools I used. And this is to say nothing of the teachers and other artists who taught and inspired me. The list of people and circumstance I could thank is literally endless.

Nonetheless, I'd explicitly would like to thank my mother (Susan Mueller) for reading drafts of this book and offering edits. I'd also like to thank the talented artist Serafima Antipova who illustrated the wonderful rooster I used on the cover. I'd also like to thank my wife Melissa for her love and loyalty. She knows better than anyone the challenges of living with me as I struggle to share my gifts creatively. And she's also listened to me cock-a-doodle-doo plenty.

☺Brian

About

I was born and have spent most of my life in Southwestern Ohio. It's the place where I currently live, work, and am proud to call home. This is also a region that many other peoples and cultures inhabited long before me. Included among those tribes native to Southern Ohio are the Adena, Hopewell, Kaskaskia, Myaamia (Miami), Osage, Shawandasse Tula (Shawanwaki, Shawnee).*

I sincerely hope within all my writing is a thread connected firmly to the fabric that encompasses those who have long called these lands home.

*Source: Native Land Digital

Discover more of my writing at:

www.BrianMueller.com

www.DigitalAlphabet.com

Also by Brian

 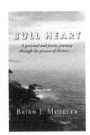  

The Bull Series

Brian's Poem of the Day Series

- -

More information about these titles is available at

www.DigitalAlphabet.com.

You can also find them at online retailers or order

them through your favorite bookstore!

Notes

These pages are for your thoughts and poems...